Salad Cookbook: Delicious Hi
Salad Recipes for Easy Wei

by **Vesela Tabakova**
Text copyright(c)2015 Vesela Tabakova

Table Of Contents

Delicious Protein-Packed Vegetarian Salads

Salads can make us live longer and better. They are known to be rich in vitamins and antioxidants and are a superb source of natural fiber. Making a nutritious vegetarian salad is relatively quick and there are thousands of ingredient combinations. You could have a different salad every day for years - the only limiting factor is your imagination!

Salads are a great way to get more fresh fruit and vegetables in your diet. Combine a variety of leaves, beans, peas, nuts, seeds, eggs and dairy into your salad and you will have an amazing protein-rich vegetarian salad that will fill you up and keep you satisfied for hours. Better still, high protein vegetarian salads will help you eat less of the unhealthy junk foods and ultimately help you lose weight.

You can start your meal with a salad, like I usually do, or you can replace a whole meal with a fresh salad.

One of the healthiest eating habits you can adopt, and one of the simplest, is eating a protein and fiber packed salad every day. This simple change to your diet can pay off with plenty of health benefits.

Spinach and Barley Salad

Serves: 4

Ingredients:

2/3 cup quick-cooking barley

3 cups finely cut spinach leaves

7-8 cherry tomatoes, halved

1 cup crumbled feta cheese

2-3 green onions, cut

for the dressing:

3 tbsp olive oil

2 tbsp white wine vinegar

1 garlic clove, crushed

salt and black pepper, to taste

Directions:

Cook barley according to package instructions

Whisk the dressing ingredients in a small bowl until smooth. Season with salt and pepper to taste.

Combine barley, spinach, tomatoes, cheese, and onions in a salad bowl. Drizzle with the dressing, toss to combine and serve.

Roasted Leek and Sweet Potato Salad

Serves: 5

Ingredients:

1 lb sweet potato, unpeeled, cut into 1 inch pieces

3-4 leeks, trimmed and cut into 1 inch slices

a handful of baby spinach leaves

1 cup watercress, rinsed, patted dry and separated from roots

1/2 cup roasted pumpkin seeds

1 tbsp dried mint

2 tbsp olive oil

2 tbsp lemon juice

Directions:

Preheat oven to 350 F. Line a baking tray with baking paper and place the sweet potato and leeks on it. Drizzle with olive oil and sprinkle with mint. Toss to coat. Roast for 20 minutes or until tender.

Place roasted vegetables, baby spinach and watercress in a salad bowl and stir. Add in the pumpkin seed, sprinkle with lemon juice, and serve.

Mediterranean Avocado Salad

Serves: 5

Ingredients:

1 avocado, peeled, halved and cut into cubes

1 cup grape tomatoes

1 cup radishes, sliced

2 tbsp drained capers, rinsed

1 large cucumber, quartered and sliced

3 tbsp sunflower seeds

½ cup green olives, pitted, halved

½ cup black olives, pitted, sliced

7-8 fresh basil leaves, torn

2 tbsp olive oil

2 tbsp red wine vinegar

salt and pepper, to taste

Directions:

Place avocado, cucumber, tomatoes, radishes, olives, capers and basil in a large salad bowl.

Toss to combine then sprinkle with the sunflower seeds, vinegar and olive oil. Season with salt and pepper, toss again and serve.

Avocado and Cucumber Salad

Serves: 5

Ingredients:

2 avocados, peeled, halved and sliced

2-3 green onions, finely cut

1 cucumber, halved, sliced

1/2 cup canned black beans

for the dressing:

2 tbsp olive oil

3 tbsp lemon juice

1 tbsp Dijon mustard

1/2 cup finely cut dill leaves

salt and pepper, to taste

Directions:

Combine avocado, cucumber, beans and green onions in a deep salad bowl.

Whisk olive oil, lemon juice, dill and mustard until smooth, then drizzle over the salad.

Season with salt and pepper to taste, toss to combine and serve.

Warm Vitamin Salad

Serves: 4

Ingredients:

7 oz cauliflower, cut into florets

7 oz baby Brussels sprouts, trimmed

7 oz broccoli, cut into florets

1/2 cup chopped leeks

for the dressing:

1/2 cup Greek Yogurt

2 tbsp olive oil

1/2 tsp ginger powder

1/2 cup parsley leaves, very finely cut

Directions:

Cook cauliflower, broccoli and Brussels sprouts in a steamer basket over boiling water for 10 minutes or until just tender. Refresh under cold water for a minute and set aside in a deep salad bowl.

Whisk the yogurt, olive oil and ginger powder in a small bowl. Add in salt and pepper to taste; pour over the salad.

Top with parsley and serve.

Kale Salad with Creamy Tahini Dressing

Serves 4

Ingredients:

1 head kale

2 cucumbers, peeled and diced

1 avocado, peeled and diced

1 red onion, finely chopped

1 cup cherry tomatoes, halved

for the dressing

1/3 cup tahini

1/2 cup water

2 garlic cloves, minced

3 tbsp lemon juice

4 tbsp olive oil

salt and freshly ground black pepper, to taste

Directions:

Prepare the dressing by whisking all ingredients.

Place all salad ingredients in bowl and toss with the dressing.

Season to taste with black pepper and salt.

Tomato and Blue Cheese Salad

Serves 4

Ingredients:

3-4 large tomatoes, sliced

1 red onion, sliced

2/3 cup crumbled blue cheese

2-3 fresh mint leaves

2 tbsp olive oil

Directions:

Place the tomatoes in a shallow salad bowl. Add the onion and blue cheese. Season with salt to taste.

Drizzle olive oil over the salad and garnish with the fresh mint leaves.

Zucchini Salad with Yogurt

Serves 4

Ingredients:

3 medium zucchinis, coarsely grated

1 cup Greek yogurt

2/3 cup crushed walnuts

2 garlic cloves, chopped

2 tbsp olive oil

1 tsp paprika

1 tbsp dried mint

1/2 cup fresh dill, finely cut

salt, to taste

Directions:

Grate zucchinis and squeeze them by hand to drain excessive juice.

Heat olive oil in a pan and gently cook zucchinis, stirring, for 4-5 minutes or until tender. Stir in paprika and set aside to cool down.

When zucchinis have cooled, add in garlic, walnuts, dill, mint and salt. Stir to combine well and add in yogurt. Stir again and serve cold.

Artichoke and Bean Salad with Lemon Mint Dressing

Serves 5

Ingredients:

1 can white beans, drained

2/3 cup podded broad beans

4 marinated artichoke hearts, quartered

2/3 cup diced green bell pepper

for the dressing:

3 tbsp olive oil

3 tbsp lemon juice

1 tsp dried mint

1 tsp chia seeds

5-6 fresh mint leaves, very finely cut

salt and pepper, to taste

Boil the broad beans in unsalted water for 3-4 minutes or until tender. Drain and hold under running cold water for a few minutes. Combine with the canned beans, bell peppers and quartered marinated artichoke hearts in a deep salad bowl.

In a small bowl, mix olive oil, lemon juice, chia seeds, dried mint and fresh mint. Whisk until smooth. Add in salt and pepper and pour over salad. Toss gently to combine and serve.

Artichoke and Mushroom Salad

Serves: 4-5

Ingredients:

1 oz can artichoke hearts, drained, quartered

7-8 white button mushrooms, chopped

1 red pepper, chopped

2 hard boiled eggs, peeled and quartered

1/3 cup chopped black olives

1 tbsp capers

3 tbsp lemon juice

2 tbsp olive oil

salt and pepper, to taste

Directions:

Place the artichokes and mushrooms in a large salad bowl and stir to mix well. Add in the eggs, olives, capers and red pepper and toss to combine.

In a small bowl, whisk the lemon juice and olive oil until smooth. Pour over the salad, toss and serve.

Warm Quinoa Salad

Serves 6

Ingredients:

1 cup quinoa

2 cups water

1/2 cup green beans, frozen

1/2 cup sweet corn, frozen

1/2 cup carrots, diced

1/2 cup black olives, pitted

2 garlic cloves, crushed

2 tbsp soy sauce

2 tbsp fresh dill, finely cut

3 tbsp lemon juice

2 tbsp olive oil

Directions:

Wash quinoa with lots of water. Strain it and cook it according to package directions. When ready set aside in a large salad bowl.

Stew green beans, sweet corn and carrots in a little olive oil until tender. Add to quinoa. In a smaller bowl, combine soy sauce, lemon juice, dill and garlic and pour over the warm salad. Add salt and pepper to taste and serve.

Quinoa and Black Bean Salad

Serves 6

Ingredients:

1 cup quinoa

1 cup black beans, cooked, rinsed and drained

1/2 cup sweet corn, cooked

1 red bell pepper, deseeded and chopped

4 spring onions, chopped

1 garlic clove, crushed

1 tbsp dry mint

2 tbsp lemon juice

1 tbsp apple cider vinegar

4 tbsp cup olive oil

Directions:

Rinse quinoa in a fine sieve under cold running water until water runs clear.

Put quinoa in a pot with two cups of water. Bring to a boil, then reduce heat, cover and simmer for fifteen minutes or until water is absorbed and quinoa is tender. Fluff quinoa with a fork and set aside to cool.

Put beans, corn, bell pepper, spring onions and garlic in a bowl and toss with vinegar and black pepper to taste. Add quinoa and toss well again.

In a separate bowl whisk together lemon juice, salt and olive oil and drizzle over salad. Toss well and serve.

Roasted Vegetable Quinoa Salad

Serves 6

Ingredients:

2 zucchinis, cut into bite sized pieces

1 eggplant cut into bite sized pieces

3 roasted red peppers, cut into bite sized pieces

4-5 small white mushrooms, whole

1 cup quinoa

1/2 cup olive oil

1 tbsp apple cider vinegar

1/2 tsp savory

salt and pepper to taste

7 oz feta, crumbled

Directions:

Toss the zucchinis, mushrooms and eggplant in half the olive oil, salt and pepper. Place onto a baking sheet in a single layer and bake in a preheated 350 F oven for 30 minutes flipping once. Wash well, strain and cook the quinoa following package directions.

Prepare the dressing from the remaining olive oil, apple cider vinegar, savory, salt and pepper.

In a big bowl combine quinoa, roasted zucchinis, eggplant, mushrooms, roasted red peppers, and feta. Toss the dressing into the salad.

Quinoa with Oven Roasted Tomatoes and Pesto

Serves 6

Ingredients :

for the salad

1 cup dry quinoa

2 cups water

1 cup cherry tomatoes, for roasting

1/2 cup cherry tomatoes, fresh

1 avocado, cut into chunks

1/2 cup black olives, pitted

1 cup mozzarella cheese, cut into bite size pieces

for the pesto

1 clove garlic, chopped

1/2 tsp salt

1/2 cup walnuts, toasted

1 cup basil leaves

1 tbsp lemon juice

1 tbsp mustard

4-6 tbsp olive oil

1 tsp savory

Directions:

Preheat the oven to 350 F. Line a baking sheet with foil. Make sure the tomatoes are completely dry, then drizzle with olive oil and savory and toss to coat them all. Bake the tomatoes for about twenty minutes, flipping once, until they are brown. Sprinkle with salt.

Rinse quinoa very well in a fine mesh strainer under running water; set aside to drain. Place two cups of water and quinoa in a large saucepan over medium-high heat. Bring to the boil then reduce heat to low. Simmer for fifteen minutes. Set aside, covered, for ten minutes and fluff with a fork.

Make the pesto by placing garlic, walnuts and 1/2 teaspoon salt in a food processor. Add basil, mustard and lemon juice and blend in batches until smooth. Add oil, one tablespoon at a time, processing in between, until the pesto is lightened and creamy. For an even lighter texture you can add two tablespoons of water. Taste for salt and add more if you like.

In a large mixing bowl, gently mix the quinoa with the tomatoes, avocado, olives and mozzarella pieces. Spoon in the pesto and toss to distribute it evenly.

Cucumber Quinoa Salad

Serves 6

Ingredients:

1 cup quinoa, rinsed

2 cups water

1 large cucumber, diced

1/2 cup black olives, pitted

2 tbsp lemon juice

2 tbsp olive oil

1 bunch fresh dill, finely cut

Directions:

Wash quinoa very well in a fine mesh strainer under running water and set aside to drain. Place quinoa and two cups of cold water in a saucepan over high heat and bring to the boil.

Reduce heat to low and simmer for fifteen minutes. Set aside, covered, for ten minutes, then transfer to a large bowl. Add finely cut dill, cucumber and olives.

Prepare a dressing from the lemon juice, olive oil, salt and pepper. Add it to the salad and toss to combine.

Fresh Vegetable Quinoa Salad

Serves 6

Ingredients:

1 cup quinoa

2 cups water

a bunch of fresh onions, chopped

2 green peppers, chopped

1/2 cup black olives, pitted and chopped

2 tomatoes, diced

1 cup raw sunflower seeds

3 tbsp olive oil

4 tbsp fresh lemon juice

1 tbsp dried mint

Directions:

Prepare the dressing by combining olive oil, lemon juice, and dried mint in a small bowl and mixing it well. Place the dressing in the refrigerator until ready to use.

Wash well and cook quinoa according to package directions. When it is ready leave it aside for ten minutes, then transfer it to a large bowl. Add the diced peppers, finely cut fresh onions, olives and diced tomatoes stirring until mixed well.

Stir the dressing (it will have separated by this point) and add it to the salad, tossing to evenly coat. Add salt and pepper to taste and sprinkle with sunflower seeds.

Warm Mushroom Quinoa Salad

Serves 4-5

Ingredients:

1 cup quinoa

2 cups vegetable broth

1 tbsp sunflower oil

2-3 spring onions, chopped

2 garlic cloves, chopped

10 white mushrooms, sliced

1-2 springs of fresh rosemary

1/2 cup dried tomatoes, chopped

2 tbsp olive oil

salt and freshly ground pepper

1/2 bunch fresh parsley

Directions:

Wash well the quinoa in plenty of cold water, strain it and put it in a saucepan. Add vegetable broth and bring to the boil. Lower heat and simmer for ten minutes until the broth is absorbed.

Heat oil in a frying pan and sauté onions for 2-3 minutes. Add garlic and sauté for another minute. Add sliced mushrooms and season with salt and pepper. Finally, add the rosemary. Stir fry the mushrooms until soft.

Mix well the cooked quinoa with the mushrooms and tomatoes. Serve sprinkled with fresh parsley.

Mediterranean Buckwheat Salad

Serves 4-5

Ingredients:

1 cup buckwheat groats

1 3/4 cups water

1 small red onion, finely chopped

1/2 cucumber, diced

1 cup cherry tomatoes, halved

1 yellow bell pepper, chopped

a bunch parsley, finely cut

1 preserved lemon, finely chopped

1 cup chickpeas, cooked or canned, drained

juice of half lemon

1 tsp dried basil

2 tbsp olive oil

salt and black pepper, to taste

Directions:

Heat a large, dry saucepan and toast the buckwheat for about three minutes. Boil the water and add it carefully to the buckwheat.

Cover, reduce heat and simmer until buckwheat is tender and all liquid is absorbed (5-7 minutes). Remove from heat, fluff with a fork and set aside to cool.

Mix the buckwheat with the chopped onion, bell pepper, cucumber, cherry tomatoes, parsley, preserved lemon and chickpeas in a salad bowl.

Whisk the lemon juice, olive oil and basil, season with salt and pepper to taste, then pour over the salad and stir. Serve at room temperature.

Spicy Buckwheat Vegetable Salad

Serves 4-5

Ingredients:

1 cup buckwheat groats

2 cups vegetable broth

2 tomatoes, diced

1/2 cup spring onions, chopped

1/2 cup parsley leaves, finely chopped

1/2 cup fresh mint leaves, very finely chopped

1/2 yellow bell pepper, chopped

1 cucumber, peeled and cut into 1/4-inch cubes

1/2 cup cooked or canned brown lentils, drained

1/4 cup freshly squeezed lemon juice

1 tsp hot pepper sauce

salt, to taste

Directions:

Heat a large, dry saucepan and toast the buckwheat for about three minutes. Boil the vegetable broth and add it carefully to the buckwheat. Cover, reduce heat and simmer until buckwheat is tender and all liquid is absorbed (five-seven minutes). Remove from heat, fluff with a fork and set aside to cool.

Chop all vegetables and add them together with the lentils to the buckwheat. Mix the lemon juice and remaining ingredients well and drizzle over the buckwheat mixture. Stir well to distribute the dressing evenly.

Buckwheat Salad with Asparagus and Roasted Peppers

Serves 4-5

Ingredients:

1 cup buckwheat groats

1 3/4 cups vegetable broth

1/2 lb asparagus, trimmed and cut into 1 in pieces

4 roasted red bell peppers, diced

2-3 spring onions, finely chopped

2 garlic cloves, crushed

1 tbsp red wine vinegar

3 tbsp olive oil

salt and black pepper, to taste

1/2 cup fresh parsley leaves, finely cut

Directions:

Heat a large, dry saucepan and toast the buckwheat for about three minutes. Boil the vegetable broth and add it carefully to the buckwheat. Cover, reduce heat and simmer until buckwheat is tender and all liquid is absorbed (five-seven minutes). Remove from heat, fluff with a fork and set aside to cool.

Rinse out the saucepan and then bring about an inch of water to a boil. Cook the asparagus in a steamer basket or colander, two to three minutes until tender. Transfer the asparagus in a large bowl along with the roasted peppers. Add in the spring onions, garlic, red wine vinegar, salt, pepper and olive oil. Stir to combine. Add the buckwheat to the vegetable mixture. Sprinkle with parsley and toss the salad gently. Serve at room temperature.

Roasted Broccoli Buckwheat Salad

Serves 4-5

Ingredients:

1 cup buckwheat groats

1 3/4 cups water

1 head of broccoli, cut into small pieces

1 lb asparagus, trimmed and cut into 1 in pieces

1/2 cup roasted cashews

1/2 cup basil leaves, minced

1/2 cup olive oil

2 garlic cloves, crushed

1 tsp salt

3 tbsp Parmesan cheese, grated, to serve

Directions:

Arrange vegetables on a baking sheet and drizzle with olive oil. Roast in a preheated to 350 F oven for about fifteen minutes or until tender.

Heat a large, dry saucepan and toast the buckwheat for about three minutes, or until it releases a nutty aroma. Boil the water and add it carefully to the buckwheat. Cover, reduce heat and simmer until buckwheat is tender and all liquid is absorbed (five-seven minutes). Remove from heat, fluff with a fork and set aside to cool.

Prepare the dressing by blending basil leaves, olive oil, garlic, and salt.

Toss vegetables, buckwheat and dressing together in a salad bowl. Add in cashews and serve sprinkled with Parmesan cheese.

Haloumi, Lentil and Rocket Salad

Serves 4

Ingredients:

1 cup brown lentils, cooked and drained

1 cup cherry tomatoes, halved

2 cucumbers, halved and thinly sliced

1/2 cup baby rocket leaves

1/2 red onion, finely cut

1 tbsp lemon juice

1 tsp honey

4 tbsp olive oil

6 oz haloumi, cut into slices

Directions:

Combine the lentils, tomatoes, cucumber, rocket leaves and onion in a salad bowl. Whisk together lemon juice, honey, olive oil, salt and pepper in a small bowl. Drizzle the dressing over the salad and toss to coat.

Pat the haloumi dry with a paper towel and toss in the remaining olive oil. Heat a frying pan over medium heat and cook the haloumi in batches, for one-two minutes each side or until golden. Transfer to a plate.

Divide the salad among serving plates. Top with haloumi and serve.

Brown Lentil Salad

Serves 4

Ingredients:

1 can lentils, drained and rinsed

1 red onion, thinly sliced

1 tomato, diced

1 red bell pepper, chopped

2 garlic cloves, crushed

2 tbsp lemon juice

1/3 cup parsley leaves

salt and pepper to taste

Directions:

Place lentils, red onion, tomato, bell pepper and lemon juice in a large bowl.

Season with salt and black pepper to taste. Toss to combine and sprinkle with parsley. Serve.

Avocado and Orange Salad

Serves 3

Ingredients:

2 avocados, peeled, pitted and sliced

2 oranges, peeled and sliced

2 tbsp olive oil

4 tbsp roasted cedar nuts

2 tbsp chopped parsley leaves

Directions:

Arrange avocado and orange slices in 3 plates. Sprinkle with parsley and roasted cedar nuts.

Season with salt to taste, drizzle olive oil, and serve.

Blue Cheese Iceberg Salad

Serves 6

Ingredients:

1 small iceberg salad

1 avocado, cut

1 cucumber, cut

1 red onion, cut

1/2 cup walnuts, raw

5.5 oz blue cheese, coarsely crumbled

¼ cup orange juice

3 tbsp olive oil

1 tbsp honey

salt

Directions:

Tear the iceberg lettuce or cut it in thin strips. Toss it in a medium salad bowl together with the other vegetables. Add the coarsely crumbled blue cheese.

Whisk together honey, orange juice, olive oil and salt and drizzle over the salad. Toss in the walnuts and serve.

Apple, Walnut and Radicchio Salad

Serves 4

Ingredients:

2 radicchio, trimmed, finely shredded

2 apples, quartered and thinly sliced

4 spring onions, chopped

1/2 cup walnuts, roasted

1 tbsp mustard

1 tbsp lemon juice

1/3 cup olive oil

Directions:

Prepare the dressing by combining mustard, lemon juice and olive oil.

Place walnuts on an oven tray and roast in a preheated to 400 F oven for three-four minutes or until brown.

Mix radicchio, apples, onions and walnuts in a large salad bowl. Add the dressing and toss to combine.

Apple, Celery and Walnut Salad

Serves 4

Ingredients:

4 apples, quartered, cores removed, thinly sliced

1 celery rib, thinly sliced

1/2 cup walnuts, chopped

2 tbsp raisins

1 large red onion, thinly sliced

3 tbsp apple cider vinegar

2 tbsp sunflower oil

Directions:

Mix vinegar, oil, salt and pepper in a small bowl. Whisk until well combined.

Combine apples, celery, walnuts, raisins and onion in a bigger salad bowl. Drizzle with dressing and toss gently.

Greek Chickpea Salad

Serves 4

Ingredients:

1 cup canned chickpeas, drained and rinsed

1 spring onion, finely cut

1 small cucumber, deseeded and diced

2 green bell peppers, diced

2 tomatoes, diced

2 tsp chopped fresh parsley

1 tsp capers, drained and rinsed

juice of half lemon

2 tbsp olive oil

1 tbsp balsamic vinegar

salt and pepper, to taste

a pinch of dried oregano

Directions:

In a medium bowl toss together the chickpeas, spring onion, cucumber, bell pepper, tomato, parsley, capers and lemon juice.

In a smaller bowl stir together the remaining ingredients and pour over the chickpea salad.

Toss well to coat and allow to marinate, stirring occasionally, for at least 1 hour before serving.

Snow White Salad

Serves 4

Ingredients:

1 large or two small cucumbers-fresh or pickled

4 cups of plain yogurt

1/2 cup of crushed walnuts

2-3 cloves garlic, crushed

1/2 bunch of dill

3 tbsp sunflower oil

salt, to taste

Directions:

Strain the yogurt in a piece of cheesecloth or a clean white dishtowel. You can suspend it over a bowl or the sink.

Peel and dice the cucumbers, place in a large bowl. Add the crushed walnuts and the crushed garlic, the oil and the finely chopped dill. Scoop the drained yogurt into the bowl and stir well.

Add salt to the taste, cover with cling film, and put in the fridge for at least an hour so the flavors can mix well.

Asian Coleslaw

Serves 4

Ingredients:

for the salad

1/2 Chinese cabbage, shredded

1 cup cooked quinoa

1 green bell pepper, sliced into thin strips

1 carrot, cut into thin strips

4 green onions, chopped

for the dressing

3 tbsp lemon juice

3 tbsp soy sauce

3 tbsp sweet chilly sauce

Directions:

Remove any damaged outer leaves and rinse cabbage. Holding cabbage from the base and starting at the opposite end shred leaves thinly.

Combine the vegetables and quinoa in a salad bowl.

Prepare the dressing by mixing lemon juice, soy sauce and sweet chilly sauce. Pour it over the salad and toss well.

Asian Carrot and Sprout Salad

Serves 4

Ingredients:

2 carrots, peeled and cut into ribbons

6 oz snow peas, trimmed, thinly sliced diagonally

2 cucumbers, cut into ribbons

1 cup bean sprouts, trimmed

1/2 cup snow pea sprouts, trimmed

1 tbsp sesame seeds, toasted

2 tbsp sunflower oil

2 tbsp rice wine vinegar

2 tsp sesame oil

1 tsp honey

Directions:

Mix sunflower oil, vinegar, sesame oil and honey and whisk to combine. Season with salt and pepper.

Put the carrot and snow peas in boiling water and let stand for two minutes or until snow peas turn bright green.

Drain, rinse under cold water and place in a salad bowl. Add in cucumber, beans sprouts, snow pea sprouts and sesame seeds.

Drizzle with dressing, toss to combine, and serve.

Shredded Egg Salad

Serves 4

Ingredients:

3 large hard boiled eggs, shredded

2-3 spring onions, finely cut

2-3 garlic cloves, crushed

4 tbsp mayonnaise

1 tbsp mustard

1 tbsp yogurt

1 salt and pepper, to taste

Directions:

Peel the shell off of the eggs. Shred the eggs in a medium salad bowl. Mix in the remaining ingredients. Serve chilled.

Chickpea and Roasted Root Vegetable Salad

Serves 5

Ingredients:

4 potatoes, peeled and quartered

3 onions, quartered

5-6 parsnips, peeled and halved lengthwise

a bunch of baby carrots, peeled and halved lengthwise

1 can chickpeas, drained

1 tbsp oregano

3 tbsp olive oil

for the dressing

1/2 cup yogurt

2 tbsp Dijon mustard

1 garlic clove, chopped

Directions:

Arrange the vegetables on a lined baking sheet. Season with salt, pepper and oregano and sprinkle with olive oil.

Roast in a 500 F oven until golden, about 35 minutes.

Add in the chickpeas; toss to combine, and roast for 15 minutes or until the chickpeas are beginning to crisp.

Whisk the dressing ingredients in a bowl. Divide the vegetables and chickpeas in 5 plates. Top with the yogurt-mustard mixture and serve.

Fresh Greens Salad

Serves 8

Ingredients:

1 head red leaf lettuce, rinsed, dried and chopped

1 head green leaf lettuce, rinsed, dried, and chopped

1 head endive, rinsed, dried and chopped

1 cup frisee lettuce leaves, rinsed, dried, and chopped

1 cup crumbled feta cheese

3 leaves fresh basil, chopped

3 sprigs fresh mint, chopped

4 tbsp olive oil

2 tbsp lemon juice

1 tbsp honey

salt, to taste

Directions:

Place the red and green leaf lettuce, frisee lettuce, endive, basil, and mint into a large salad bowl and toss lightly to combine. Add the crumbled feta cheese.

Prepare the dressing from lemon juice, olive oil and honey and pour over the salad. Season with salt to taste.

Simple Broccoli Salad

Serves 4

Ingredients:

14 oz fresh broccoli, cut into florets

3-4 green onions, finely cut

1/3 cup raisins

1/3 cup sunflower seeds

1/2 cup yogurt

2 tbsp mayonnaise

1/3 cup orange juice

Directions:

Combine broccoli, onions, raisins, and sunflower seeds in a medium salad bowl.

In a smaller bowl, whisk together the yogurt, orange juice, and mayonnaise until blended. Pour over the broccoli mixture and toss to coat.

Caprese Salad

Serves 6

Ingredients:

4 tomatoes, sliced

5.5 oz mozzarella cheese, sliced

10 fresh basil leaves

3 tbsp olive oil

2 tbsp balsamic vinegar

salt, to taste

Directions:

Slice the tomatoes and mozzarella, then layer the tomato slices, basil leaves and mozzarella slices on a plate.

Drizzle olive oil and balsamic vinegar over the salad and serve.

High Protein Bulgarian Green Salad

Serves 4

Ingredients:

1 green lettuce, washed and drained

1 cucumber, sliced

a bunch of radishes

3 hard boiled eggs, peeled and sliced

a bunch of spring onions

juice of half lemon or 2 tbsp of white wine vinegar

3 tbsp olive oil

salt, to taste

Directions:

Cut the lettuce into thin strips. Slice the cucumber and the radishes as thinly as possible and chop the spring onions.

Mix all the salad ingredients in a large bowl, add the egg and toss to combine. Stir in lemon juice and oil and season with salt to taste.

Green Superfood Salad

Serves 6

Ingredients:

4 cups mixed green salad leaves

2 cups broccoli or sunflower sprouts

1 avocado, cubed

2 cucumbers, chopped

1 tbs sunflower seeds

1 tbs pumpkin seeds

2 tbsp lemon juice

3 tbsp olive oil

1/2 tsp mustard

salt and pepper, to taste

Directions:

Mix all vegetables in a big salad bowl. Toss well to combine.

Prepare the dressing by whisking together olive oil, lemon juice and mustard. Season with salt and pepper to taste. Drizzle over the salad and toss again.

Sprinkle the salad with sunflower and pumpkin seeds and serve.

Fried Zucchinis with Yogurt Sauce

Serves 4

Ingredients:

4 medium zucchinis

2 cups yogurt

3 cloves garlic, crushed

a bunch of fresh dill, chopped

1 cup sunflower oil

1 cup flour

salt

Directions:

Start by combining the garlic and chopped dill with the yogurt in a bowl. Add salt to taste and put in the fridge.

Wash and peel the zucchinis, and cut them in thin diagonal slices or in rings 1/4 in thick. Salt and leave them in a suitable bowl placing it inclined to drain away the juices.

Coat the zucchinis with flour, then fry turning on both sides until they are golden-brown (about 3 minutes on each side). Transfer to paper towels and pat dry.

Serve the zucchinis hot or cold, with the yogurt mixture on the side.

Cucumber Salad

Serves 4

Ingredients:

2 medium cucumbers, sliced

a bunch of fresh dill

1/2 cup roasted walnuts, halved

1/2 tsp dried oregano

2 cloves garlic

3 tbsp white wine, vinegar

5 tbsp olive oil

salt to taste

Directions:

Cut the cucumbers in rings and put them in a salad bowl. Add the finely cut dill, the pressed garlic and season with salt, oregano, vinegar and oil.

Mix well and serve cold.

Tomato Couscous Salad

Serves 4

Ingredients:

7 oz medium couscous

1 cup hot water

2 ripe tomatoes, diced

1/2 cup cooked white beans

1/2 red onion, finely cut

4 tbsp olive oil

4 tbsp lemon juice

1 tbsp dry mint

Directions:

Place the couscous in a large bowl. Boil water with one tablespoon of olive oil and pour over the couscous. Cover and set aside for ten minutes. Fluff couscous with a fork and when it is completely cold, stir in the tomatoes, beans, onion and dry mint.

In a separate small bowl, combine the remaining olive oil, the lemon juice and salt, add to the couscous and stir until well combined.

Red Cabbage Salad

Serves 6

Ingredients:

1 small head red cabbage, cored and chopped

1 bunch of fresh dill, finely cut

1/2 cup roasted pumpkin seeds

3 tbsp sunflower oil

3 tbsp red wine vinegar

1 tsp sugar

2 tsp salt

black pepper, to taste

Directions:

In a bowl, mix the oil, red wine vinegar, sugar and black pepper. Place the cabbage in a large glass bowl. Sprinkle the salt on top and crunch it with your hands to soften.

Pour dressing over the cabbage, and toss to coat. Sprinkle the salad with the pumpkin seeds and dill, cover it with foil, and leave in the refrigerator for half an hour before serving.

Cabbage, Carrot and Turnip Salad

Serves 4

Ingredients:

7 oz fresh white cabbage, shredded

7 oz carrots, shredded

7 oz white turnips, shredded

1/2 cup cooked quinoa

½ a bunch of parsley

2 tbsp white vinegar

3 tbsp sunflower oil

salt, to taste

Directions:

Combine first three ingredients need in a large bowl and mix well with hands. Add salt, vinegar and oil.

Stir in quinoa and sprinkle with parsley. Set aside for 5 minutes, stir and serve

Carrot Salad

Serves 4

Ingredients:

4 carrots, shredded

3 tbsp sesame seeds

1 apple, peeled, cored and shredded

2 garlic cloves, crushed

2 tbsp lemon juice

2 tbsp honey

salt and pepper, to taste

Directions:

In a bowl, combine the shredded carrots, apple, lemon juice, honey, garlic, salt and pepper. Stir in the sesame seeds.

Toss and chill before serving.

Fusilli Salad

Serves 6

Ingredients:

2 cups fusilli pasta

1 onion, chopped

1 green bell pepper, chopped

2 tomatoes, chopped

1 cup mushrooms, sliced

1 cup chopped Mozarella cheese

3 tbsp lemon juice

3 tbsp olive oil

Directions:

Cook pasta according to package directions or until al dente then rinse under cold water and drain.

In a large bowl combine pasta, onion, bell pepper, tomatoes, mushrooms and Mozzarella cheese.

Prepare the dressing from olive oil and lemon juice together with salt and pepper to taste. Pour the dressing over the salad, toss and serve chilled.

Bulgur Salad

Serves 4

Ingredients:

1 cup bulgur

2 cups boiling water

3 tablespoons olive oil

1/2 cup black olives, pitted, cut

1 tomato, chopped

1/2 cup crumbled blue cheese

2-3 fresh onions, finely cut

2 tbsp lemon zest

juice from two lemons

2 tbsp fresh mint, finely chopped

2 tbsp fresh parsley, finely chopped

salt and black pepper, to taste

Directions:

In a large salad bowl pour boiling water over bulgur. Stir in olive oil, lemon zest, lemon juice, mint and parsley and leave aside for thirty minutes.

Fluff bulgur with a fork and add the chopped tomato, onions and olives. Stir in blue cheese. Season with salt and pepper to taste and serve.

Roasted Eggplant and Pepper Salad

Serves 5-6

Ingredients:

2 medium eggplants

2 red or green bell peppers

2 tomatoes

3 cloves garlic, crushed

fresh parsley

1 cup crushed walnuts

1-2 tbsp red wine vinegar

olive oil, as needed

salt, pepper

Directions:

Wash and dry the vegetables. Prick the skin off the eggplants. Bake the eggplants, tomatoes and peppers in a pre-heated oven at 480 F for about forty minutes until the skins are well burnt. Take out of the oven and leave in a covered container for about ten minutes.

Peel the skins off and drain well the extra juices. Deseed the peppers. Cut all the vegetables into small pieces. Add the garlic and mix well with a fork or in a food processor. Stir in the walnuts.

Add olive oil, vinegar and salt to taste. Stir again. Serve cold and sprinkled with parsley.

Okra Salad with Cheese

Serves 4

Ingredients:

1.2 lb young okras

1 cup crumbled feta cheese

1/2 bunch parsley, chopped

2 hard tomatoes

3 tbsp sunflower oil

1/2 tsp black pepper

salt

Directions:

Trim okras, wash and cook in salted water. Drain and cool when tender.

In a small bowl, mix well the lemon juice and sunflower oil, salt and pepper. Pour over the okra arranged in a bowl and sprinkle with chopped parsley. Sprinkle with the crumbled cheese.

Wash tomatoes and cut them into slices, then garnish the salad with them.

Green Bean Salad

Serves 6

Ingredients:

2 cups green beans, cooked

1 onion, sliced

4 garlic cloves, crushed

1 tbsp fresh mint, chopped

1 bunch of fresh dill, finely chopped

3 tbsp olive oil

1 tbsp apple cider vinegar

salt and pepper to taste

Directions:

Place the green beans in a medium bowl and combine with onion, mint and dill.

In a smaller bowl, stir olive oil, vinegar, garlic, salt, and pepper. Drizzle over the green bean mixture and serve.

Zucchini Pasta Salad

Serves 6

Ingredients:

2 cups fusilli pasta

2 zucchinis, sliced and halved

4 tomatoes, cut

6 mushrooms, cut

1 small red onion, chopped

2 tbsp fresh basil, chopped

3.5 oz blue cheese

2 tbsp olive oil

1 tbsp lemon juice

black pepper to taste

Directions:

Cook pasta according to package directions or until al dente. Drain, rinse with cold water and drain again.

Place zucchinis, tomatoes, mushrooms and onion in large bowl. Add in pasta and mix gently.

Prepare a dressing by combining the olive oil, lemon juice, basil, blue cheese and black pepper. Pour it over the salad. Toss gently and serve.

Cheese Stuffed Tomatoes

Serves 4

Ingredients:

4 large tomatoes

9 oz feta cheese

1 tsp paprika

Directions:

Cut the top of each tomato in such a way as to be able to stuff the tomato and cover with the cap. Scoop out the seeds and central part of the tomatoes to create a hollow.

Mash the scooped out parts of the tomatoes, add to the feta cheese and stir to make a homogeneous mixture. Add paprika.

Stuff the tomatoes with the mixture and cover with the caps. Serve chilled, garnished with sprays of parsley.

Beet and Bean Sprout Salad

Serves 4

Ingredients:

7 beet greens, finely sliced

2 medium tomatoes, cut into wedges

1 cup bean sprouts, washed

2 hard boiled eggs, peeled and shredded

1 tbsp grated lemon rind

2 garlic cloves, crushed

1/2 cup lemon juice

1/2 cup olive oil

1 tsp salt

Directions:

In a large salad bowl toss together beet greens, bean sprouts and tomatoes. Stir in the eggs.

Prepare the dressing from the oil, lemon juice, lemon rind, salt and garlic and pour it over the salad.

Refrigerate for two hours to allow the flavor to develop before serving. Serve chilled.

Beet Salad with Yogurt

Serves 4

Ingredients:

3 medium beet roots

1 cup strained yogurt

1 clove of garlic, minced

1 tsp white vinegar or lemon juice

1 tbsp olive oil

¼ tsp dried mint

½ tsp salt

Directions:

Wash beets well, cut the stems, and steam in a pot or pan for 25-30 minutes or until cooked trough

When they cool down, peel dry with paper towel. Grate beets and put them in a deep bowl. Add the other ingredients and toss. Serve cold.

Spinach Stem Salad

Serves 1-2

Ingredients:

a few bunches of spinach stems

water to boil the stems

1 garlic clove, minced

lemon juice or vinegar, to taste

olive oil

salt, to taste

3 tbsp sesame seeds, to serve

Directions:

Trim the stems so that they will remain intact. Wash them very well.

Steam stems in a basket over boiling water for 2-3 minutes until wilted but not too fluffy. Place them on a plate and sprinkle with minced garlic, sesame seeds, olive oil, lemon juice, and salt.

Bulgarian Spinach Salad

Serves 4

Ingredients:

1 bag baby spinach, washed and dried

4-5 spring onions, finely chopped

1 cucumber, cut

1/2 cup walnuts, halved

2/3 cup yogurt

3 tbsp red wine vinegar

4 tbsp olive oil

salt and freshly ground black pepper, to taste

Directions:

Prepare the dressing by blending yogurt, olive oil and vinegar in a cup. Place the spinach leaves in a large salad bowl, together with the onions, cucumber and walnuts. Season to taste with black pepper and salt, stir well, and toss with the dressing.

Green Bean and Rocket Salad with Green Olive Dressing

Serves 4

Ingredients:

7 oz green beans, cut into 1 in lengths

1/2 cup baby rocket leaves

green olive dressing

1/2 cup green olives, pitted, finely chopped

4 tbsp olive oil

1 tbsp balsamic vinegar

1 tsp mustard

salt and black pepper, to taste

Directions:

Prepare the dressing by combining chopped olives, olive oil, vinegar and mustard in a small bowl and whisking lightly. Season with salt and pepper to taste.

Cook the green beans in salted boiling water until bright green and tender crisp. Drain and rinse with cold water. Drain again.

Place rocket leaves and beans in a salad bowl. Drizzle with green olive dressing and toss to combine.

Mozzarella, Tomato and Basil Couscous Salad

Serves 4

Ingredients:

4 tomatoes, diced

1 cup fresh mozzarella cheese, diced

3-4 spring onions, very finely cut

2 tbsp olive oil

1 tbsp lemon juice

salt, to taste

1/4 teaspoon fresh ground black pepper

1 garlic clove, crushed

1 cup couscous

1 1/4 cups water

1/2 cup chopped fresh basil

Directions:

In a big salad bowl combine tomatoes, mozzarella, salt, pepper, garlic, lemon juice, olive oil and spring onions. Toss everything well, cover, and marinate for half an hour.

Boil the water and pour over the couscous. Set aside for five minutes then fluff with a fork. Add couscous to the tomato mixture along with the chopped basil leaves and toss again.

Tabbouleh

Serves 6

Ingredients:

1 cup raw bulgur

2 cups boiling water

a bunch of parsley, finely cut

2 tomatoes, chopped

1/2 cup silvered almonds

3 tbsp olive oil

2 garlic cloves, minced

6-7 fresh onions, chopped

1 tbsp fresh mint leaves, chopped

juice of two lemons

salt and black pepper, to taste

Bring water and salt to a boil, then pour over bulgur. Cover and set aside for 15 minutes to steam. Drain excess water from bulgur and fluff with a fork. Leave to chill.

In a large bowl, mix together the parsley, tomatoes, almonds, olive oil, garlic, green onions and mint. Stir in the chilled bulgur and season to taste with salt, pepper and lemon juice.

High Protein Fatoush

Serves 6

Ingredients:

2 cups lettuce, washed, dried, and chopped

3 tomatoes, chopped

1 small cucumber, peeled and chopped

1 green pepper, seeded and chopped

½ cup radishes, sliced in half

1/2 cup cooked beans

1 small red onion, finely chopped

half a bunch of parsley, finely cut

2 tbsp finely chopped fresh mint

3 tbsp olive oil

4 tbsp lemon juice

salt and black pepper, to taste

Directions:

Place the lettuce, tomatoes, cucumbers, green pepper, radishes, beans, onion, parsley, and mint in a salad bowl.

Make the dressing by whisking together the olive oil with the lemon juice, a pinch of salt and some black pepper. Toss veggies together until everything is coated with dressing and serve.

Shredded Kale and Brussels Sprout Salad

Serves: 4-6

Ingredients:

20-25 Brussels sprouts, shredded

1 cup finely shredded kale

1/2 cup grated Parmesan

1 cup toasted walnuts, halved

1/2 cup dried cranberries

for the dressing:

6 tbsp olive oil

2 tbsp lemon juice

1 tbsp Dijon mustard

salt and pepper, to taste

Directions:

Shred the Brussels sprouts and kale in a food processor and toss them in a bowl. Add the toasted walnuts, cranberries and Parmesan cheese.

In a smaller bowl, whisk the dressing ingredients until smooth. Pour the dressing over the salad, stir, and serve.

FREE BONUS RECIPES: Vegetarian Superfood Soup Recipes for Easy Weight Loss and Detox

Minted Pea and Potato Soup

Serves 4

Ingredients:

1 onion, finely chopped

2 garlic cloves, finely chopped

4 cups vegetable broth

3-4 large potatoes, peeled and diced

1 lb green peas, frozen

1/3 cup mint leaves

3 tbsp olive oil

small mint leaves, to serve

Directions:

Heat oil in a large saucepan over medium-high heat and sauté onion and garlic for 5 minutes or until soft.

Add vegetable broth and bring to the boil, then add potatoes and mint. Cover, reduce heat, and cook for 15 minutes until tender. Add the peas 2 min before the end of the cooking time.

Remove from heat. Set aside to cool slightly, then blend soup, in batches, until smooth.

Return soup to saucepan over medium-low heat and cook until heated through. Season with salt and pepper.

Serve topped with mint leaves.

Brown Lentil Soup

Serves 4

Ingredients:

1 cup brown lentils

1 onion, chopped

2-3 cloves garlic, peeled

2 medium carrots, chopped

1 medium tomato, ripe

5 cups water

4 tbsp olive oil

1 ½ tsp paprika

1 tsp summer savory

Directions:

Heat oil in a deep soup pot, add the onion and carrots and sauté until golden. Add in paprika and lentils with warm water.

Bring to the boil, lower heat and simmer for 15-20 minutes. Chop the tomato and add it to the soup, together with the garlic and summer savory. Cook for 15 more minutes, add salt to taste and serve.

Moroccan Lentil Soup

Serves 8-9

Ingredients:

1 cup red lentils

1/2 cup canned chickpeas, drained

2 onions, chopped

2 cloves garlic, minced

1 cup canned tomatoes, chopped

1/2 cup canned white beans, drained

3 carrots, diced

3 celery ribs, diced

6 cups water

1 tsp ginger, grated

1 tsp ground cardamom

½ tsp ground cumin

3 tbsp olive oil

Directions:

In a large soup pot, sauté onions, garlic and ginger in olive oil, for about 5 minutes. Add in the water, lentils, chickpeas, white beans, tomatoes, carrots, celery, cardamom and cumin.

Bring to a boil for a few minutes, then simmer for ½ hour or longer, until the lentils are tender. Puree half the soup in a food processor or blender. Return the pureed soup to the pot, stir and serve.

Curried Lentil Soup

Serves 5-6

Ingredients:

1 cup dried lentils

1 large onion, finely cut

1 celery rib, chopped

1 large carrot, chopped

3 garlic cloves, chopped

1 can tomatoes, undrained

3 cups vegetable broth

1 tbsp curry powder

1/2 tsp ground ginger

Directions:

Combine all ingredients in slow cooker.

Cover and cook on low for 5-6 hours.

Blend soup to desired consistency, adding additional hot water to thin, if desired.

Simple Black Bean Soup

Serves 5-6

Ingredients:

1 cup dried black beans

5 cups vegetable broth

1 large onion, chopped

1 red pepper, chopped

1 tsp sweet paprika

1 tbsp dried mint

2 bay leaves

1 Serrano chili, finely chopped

1 tsp salt

4 tbsp fresh lime juice

1/2 cup chopped fresh cilantro

1 cup sour cream or yogurt, to serve

Directions:

Wash the beans and soak them in enough water overnight.

In a slow cooker, combine the beans and all other ingredients except for the lime juice and cilantro. Cover and cook on low for 7-8 hours.

Add salt, lime juice and fresh cilantro.

Serve with a dollop of sour cream or yogurt.

Bean and Pasta Soup

Serves 6-7

Ingredients:

1 cup small pasta, cooked

1 cup canned white beans, rinsed and drained

2 medium carrots, cut

1 cup fresh spinach, torn

1 medium onion, chopped

1 celery rib, chopped

2 garlic cloves, crushed

3 cups water

1 cup canned tomatoes, diced and undrained

1 cup vegetable broth

½ tsp rosemary

½ tsp basil

salt and pepper, to taste

Directions:

Add all ingredients except pasta and spinach into slow cooker. Cover and cook on low for 6-7 hours or high for 4 hours.

Add spinach and pasta about 30 minutes before the soup is finished cooking.

Slow Cooked Split Pea Soup

Serves 5-6

Ingredients:

1 lb dried green split peas, rinsed and drained

2 potatoes, peeled and diced

1 small onion, chopped

1 celery rib, chopped

1 carrot, chopped

2 garlic cloves, chopped

1 bay leaf

1 tsp black pepper

1/2 tsp salt

6 cups water

Grated feta cheese, to serve

Directions:

Combine all ingredients in slow cooker.

Cover and cook on low for 5-6 hours.

Discard bay leaf. Blend soup to desired consistency, adding additional hot water to thin, if desired.

Sprinkle grated feta cheese on top and serve with garlic or herb bread.

Spiced Citrus Bean Soup

Serves 6-7

Ingredients:

1 can (14 oz) white beans, rinsed and drained

2 medium carrots, cut

1 medium onion, chopped

1 tbsp gram masala

4 cups vegetable broth

1 cup coconut milk

1/2 tbsp grated ginger

juice of 1 orange

salt and pepper, to taste

1/2 cup fresh parsley leaves, finely cut, to serve

Directions:

In a large soup pot, sauté onions, carrots and ginger in olive oil, for about 5 minutes, stirring. Add gram masala and cook until just fragrant.

Add the orange juice and vegetable broth and bring to the boil. Simmer for about 10 min until the carrots are tender, then stir in the coconut milk.

Blend soup to desired consistency then add the beans and bring to a simmer. Serve sprinkled with parsley.

Slow Cooker Tuscan-style Soup

Serves 5-6

Ingredients:

1 lb potatoes, peeled and cubed

1 small onion, chopped

1 can mixed beans, drained

1 carrot, chopped

2 garlic cloves, chopped

4 cups vegetable broth

1 cups chopped kale

3 tbsp olive oil

1 bay leaf

salt and pepper, to taste

Parmesan cheese, to serve

Directions:

Heat oil in a skillet over medium heat and sauté the onion, carrot and garlic, stirring, for 2-3 minutes or until soft.

Combine all ingredients except the kale into the slow cooker. Season with salt and pepper to taste.

Cook on high for 4 hours or low for 6-7 hours. Add in kale about 30 minutes before soup is finished cooking. Serve sprinkled with Parmesan cheese.

Crock Pot Tomato Basil Soup

Serves: 5-6

Ingredients:

4 cups chopped fresh tomatoes or 27 oz can tomatoes

1/3 cup rice

3 cups water

1 large onion, diced

4 garlic cloves, minced

3 tbsp olive oil

1 tsp salt

1 tbsp dried basil

1 tbsp paprika

1 tsp sugar

½ bunch fresh parsley, to serve

Directions:

In a skillet, sauté onion and garlic for 2-3 minutes. When onions have softened, add them together with all other ingredients to the crock pot.

Cook on low for 5-7 hours, or on high for 3 1/2. Blend with an immersion blender and serve topped with fresh parsley.

About the Author

Vesela lives in Bulgaria with her family of six (including the Jack Russell Terrier). Her passion is going green in everyday life and she loves to prepare homemade cosmetic and beauty products for all her family and friends.

Vesela has been publishing her cookbooks for over a year now. If you want to see other healthy family recipes that she has published, together with some natural beauty books, you can check out her Author Page on Amazon.

Printed in Great Britain
by Amazon

23723918R00047